Metamorphic
ROCKS

CHERITON
CHILDREN'S BOOKS

Published in 2025 by **Cheriton Children's Books**
1 Bank Drive West, Shrewsbury, Shropshire, SY3 9DJ, UK

© Copyright 2025 Cheriton Children's Books

First Edition

Author: Sarah Eason
Designer: Paul Myerscough
Editor: Deborah Jones
Proofreader: Katie Dicker

Picture credits: Cover: Collaborate; Inside: p1: Shutterstock/Astudio, p4: Shutterstock/Ralf Geithe, p5: Shutterstock/Withan Tor, p6: Shutterstock/Vadim Sadovski, p7: Shutterstock/Himanshu Saraf, p8: Shutterstock/Vasily Gureev, p9: Shutterstock/Namu Zip, p10b: Shutterstock/Serge Skiba, p10t: Shutterstock/Rattachon Angmanee, p12: Shutterstock/Puripat Lertpunyaroj, p13: Shutterstock/Bjoern Wylezich, p14: Shutterstock/BlueRingMedia, p15: Shutterstock/BlueRingMedia, p16: Shutterstock/KrimKate, p17: Shutterstock/Lenar Musin, p18: Shutterstock/VicPhotoria, p19: Shutterstock/Artem Gorlanov, p20: Shutterstock/Andrew Chisholm, p21: Shutterstock/Anna Dickie, p22b: Shutterstock/A Shot of Bliss, p22t: Shutterstock/Yes058 Montree Nanta, p24: Shutterstock/AlexAnton, p25: Shutterstock/Karamysh, p26b: Shutterstock/Alessandro Colle, p26t: Shutterstock/Milart, p28: Shutterstock/Trygve Finkelsen, p29: Shutterstock/Marc Ward, p30b: Shutterstock/Melissaberry, p30t: Shutterstock/www.sandatlas.org, p32: Shutterstock/KrimKate, p33: Shutterstock/Wirestock Creators, p34b: Shutterstock/Sergio Shumoff, p34t: Shutterstock/Vvoe, p36: Shutterstock/Jon Bilous, p37: Shutterstock/Dibrova, p38b: Shutterstock/Jacob Boomsma, p38t: Shutterstock/Yes058 Montree Nanta, p40: Shutterstock/Harry Beugelink, p41: Shutterstock/Blueplanet97, p42t: Shutterstock/Wawritto, p43: Shutterstock/Evgeny Haritonov.

Printed in China

Please visit our website,
www.cheritonchildrensbooks.com
to see more of our high-quality books.

CONTENTS

Chapter 1

Our Rocky World

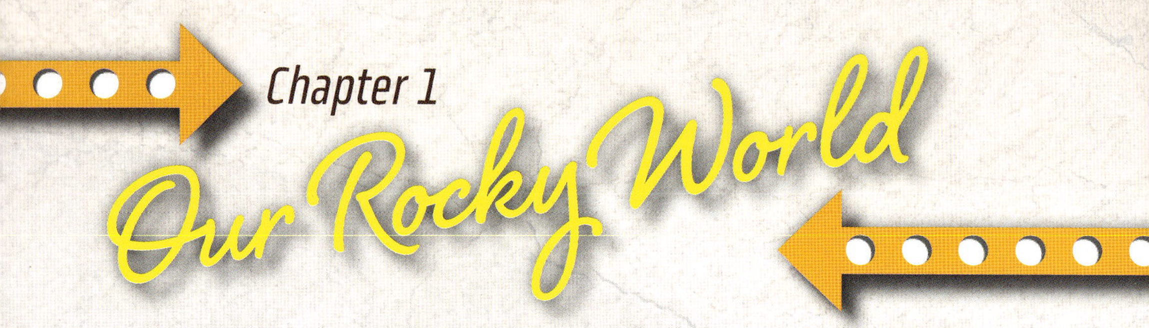

Our planet is made almost entirely of rock. It has a small metal core at its center, but the remaining 85 percent of it is rock—and that's why it is so easy to find many amazing rocks on Earth.

All Change

Although the rocky surface of our planet may seem stable, it is being reshaped and reformed all the time. Sometimes, changes to its surface can happen quickly. For example, because of a natural disaster such as a landslide or **earthquake**. Most of the time, the changes to Earth's rocky surface happen very, very slowly—so slowly that we hardly notice them. Over a very long period, surface rocks are broken down to make way for new rocks. This is part of a never-ending cycle called the rock cycle.

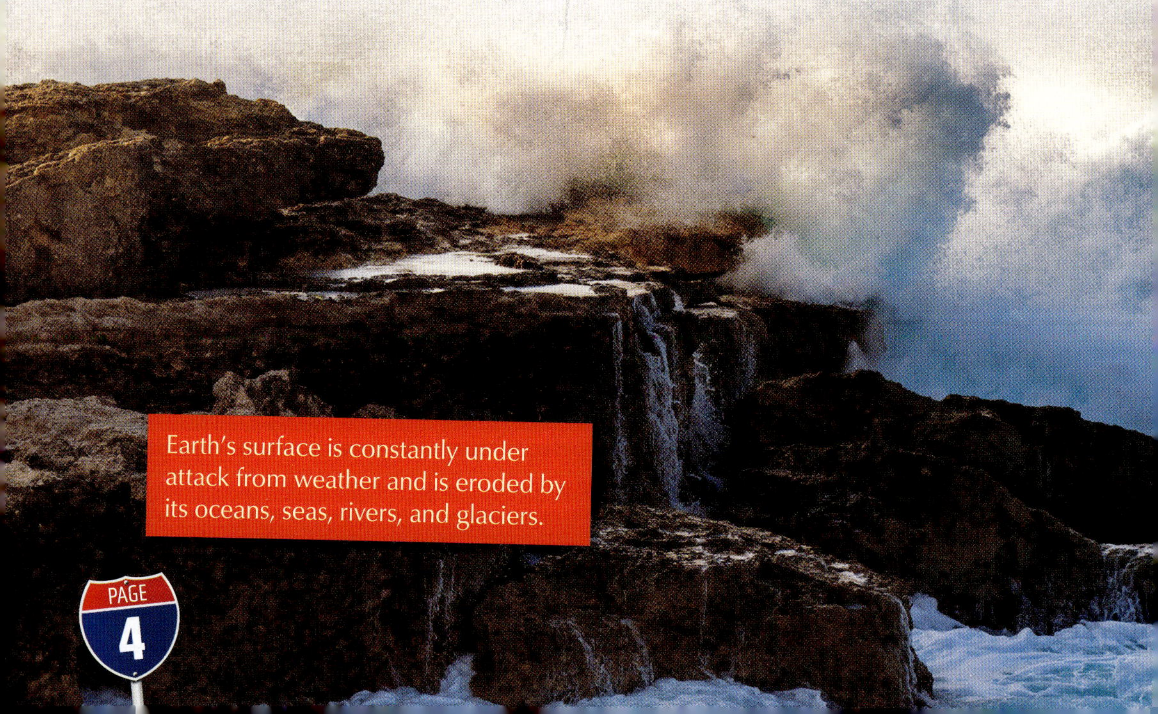

Earth's surface is constantly under attack from weather and is eroded by its oceans, seas, rivers, and glaciers.

Earth's Rock Cycle

The rock cycle is a process by which one type of rock changes into another type of rock. Earth has three main types of rock: igneous rock, metamorphic rock, and sedimentary rock. Each can change into another type when affected by temperature, **weathering**, and **pressure**.

How Rock Changes

When heated deep underground, rocks turn into liquid rock. We call this melted rock magma. When rocks are worn away by weathering or erosion, they break into smaller pieces called sediment. Rock can also be squeezed under great pressure, which also forces it to change.

Understanding Rock Types

Igneous rock is magma that has cooled and hardened. This can happen above or below the ground. Igneous rock changes by melting into magma, eroding into sediment, or being pressed so tightly that it becomes metamorphic rock.

Metamorphic rock began life as igneous or sedimentary rock that was then heated and squeezed. Metamorphic rock can change again by eroding into sediment or melting into magma.

Sedimentary rock is made up of squashed sediments from other rocks, plus the remains of living things. It can erode back into sediment, be squeezed into metamorphic rock, or melted into magma.

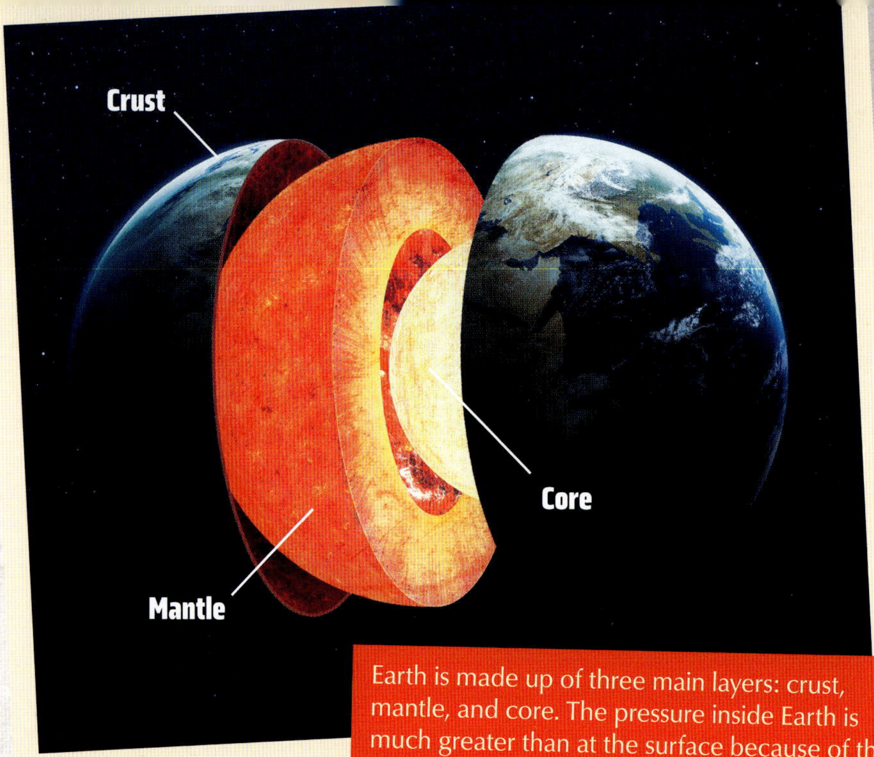

Earth is made up of three main layers: crust, mantle, and core. The pressure inside Earth is much greater than at the surface because of the downward push of millions of tons of rock above.

Look Inside Earth

To understand the rock cycle and why rock is so affected by temperature, weathering, and pressure, we need to first look at the structure of Earth.

Earth looks solid and immovable at the surface, but inside are layers that are not at all like the surface. In fact, Earth is made up of three very different parts.

Crust: This is the outer part of our planet. It is the section on which we live. It is up to 44 miles (70 km) thick and is broken up into enormous parts, called plates.

Mantle: This mostly solid layer moves around and is about 1,800 miles (2,900 km) thick. Earth's plates float on the mantle.

Core: This is the hottest part of our planet and it forms the center of Earth. The center of the core reaches nearly 12,000 degrees Fahrenheit (6,700 °C), hot enough to keep it permanently molten, or liquid.

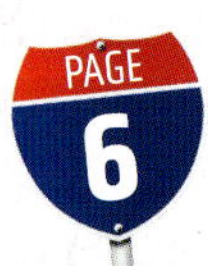

Rock Recycling

During the rock cycle, new rock material can rise to the surface from deep within Earth. But most surface rocks are made from existing rock that is continually recycled. For example, as a rock is weathered, a grain within it may be loosened. That grain may then become part of another rock. It will then be weathered and separated from that rock, and form part of a new rock, repeatedly.

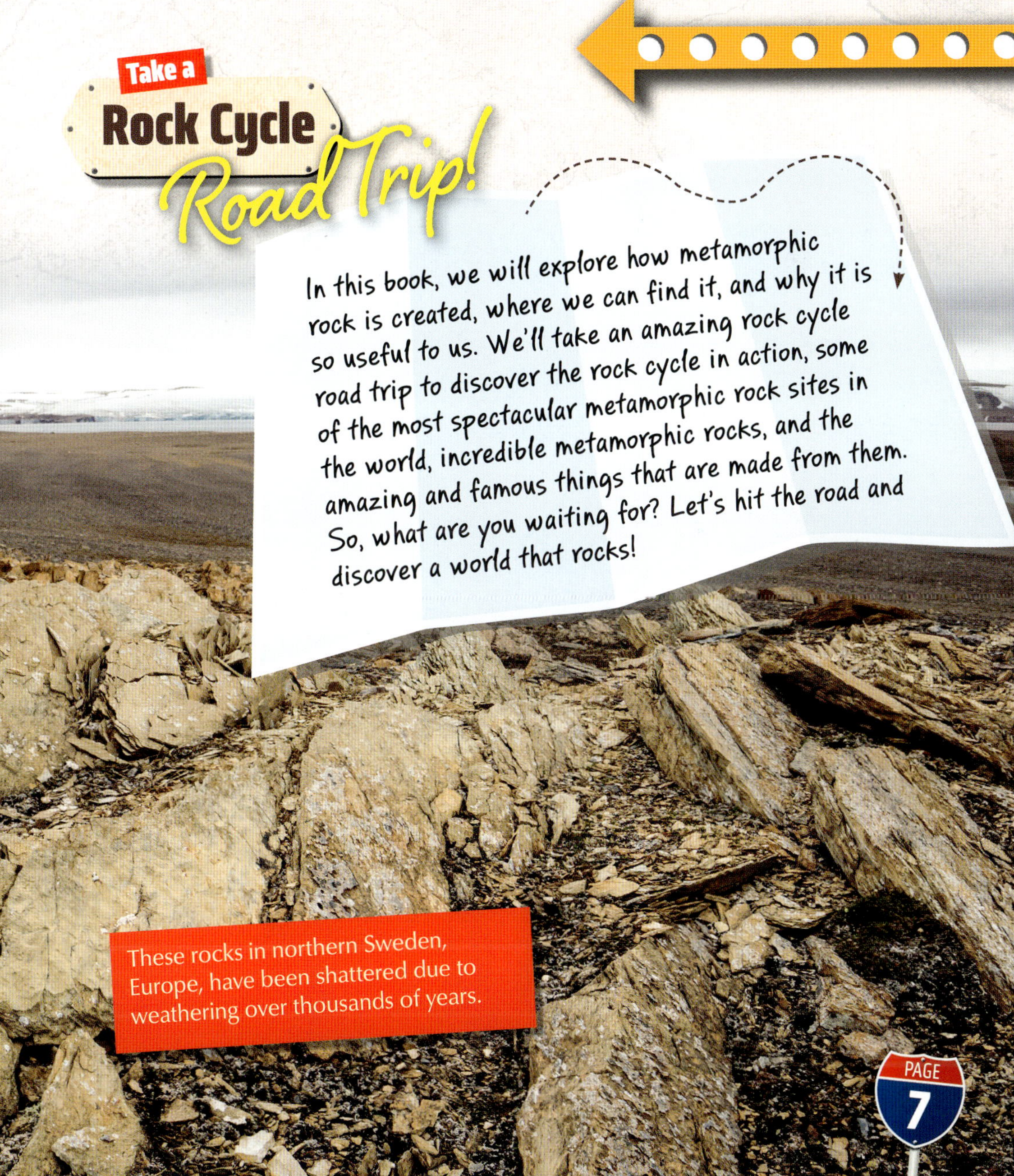

In this book, we will explore how metamorphic rock is created, where we can find it, and why it is so useful to us. We'll take an amazing rock cycle road trip to discover the rock cycle in action, some of the most spectacular metamorphic rock sites in the world, incredible metamorphic rocks, and the amazing and famous things that are made from them. So, what are you waiting for? Let's hit the road and discover a world that rocks!

These rocks in northern Sweden, Europe, have been shattered due to weathering over thousands of years.

New Rock from Old

Metamorphic means "a change in form." These rocks are so named because they are formed from igneous or sedimentary rock. Most of these changes occur deep beneath Earth's surface.

Going Up, Moving Down

Sometimes, incredible **collisions** happen on Earth. They take place at the points where Earth's plates meet. The plates move incredibly slowly. Sometimes, they collide. When this happens, the edges of the plates can crumple into giant mountains in a process that takes millions of years. Sometimes, the plates slide against each other, and this action causes earthquakes. Other times, plates dip beneath each other. When that happens, the rocks are carried underground where the heat and pressure deep within Earth's crust changes them into metamorphic rocks.

The Himalayas in Asia contain many metamorphic rocks, including migmatite, schist, phyllite, gneiss, and amphibolite.

Take a Rock Cycle Road Trip!

The Himalayan mountain range was formed when plates collided incredibly slowly millions of years ago —and it's the first stop on our road trip. Head this way!

ROCK STOP! THE HIMALAYAN MOUNTAIN RANGE, ASIA

The Himalayas are made from more than 100 mountains that are all taller than 24,000 feet (7,300 m). The range includes Mount Everest, the tallest mountain on Earth. The Himalayan range is also one of the youngest mountain ranges on Earth. It formed 50 million years ago when two plates collided and forced rock upward into the mountain range we see today.

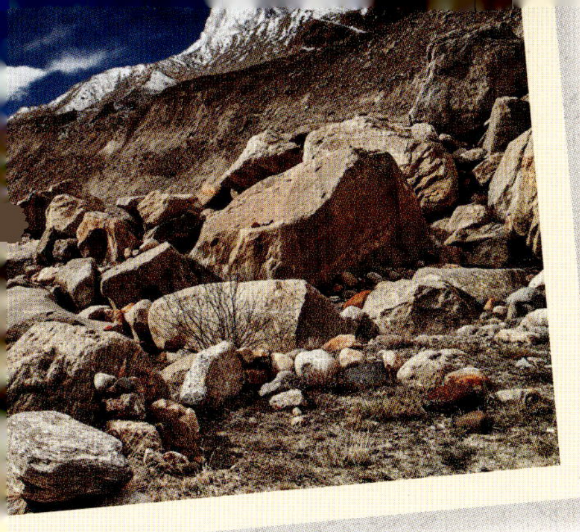

A World That Rocks!

Many different rocks cover Earth's surface, forming features such as mountains and valleys. All these rocks have something in common because they are made from **raw materials**. Those raw materials are called **minerals**, and each is made from one or more types of **elements**.

Rock Clues

Metamorphic rocks often look different from the rocks from which they formed because they contain different minerals. However, they are still made up of the same elements as the original rock. The elements in metamorphic rocks give us clues about the types of rocks they once were.

The Metamorphic Stars

There are many metamorphic rocks on Earth. Some of the best known are marble, quartzite, amphibolite, gneiss, phyllite, soapstone, schist, and slate.

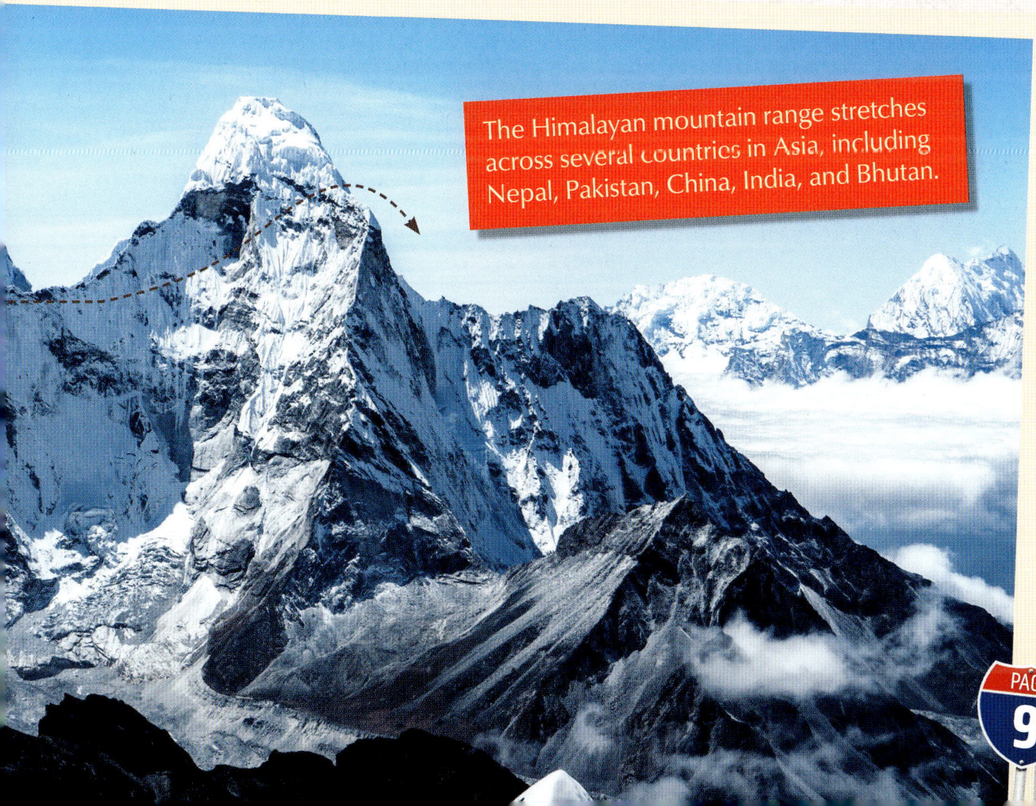

The Himalayan mountain range stretches across several countries in Asia, including Nepal, Pakistan, China, India, and Bhutan.

SCHIST

What a Rock Star!

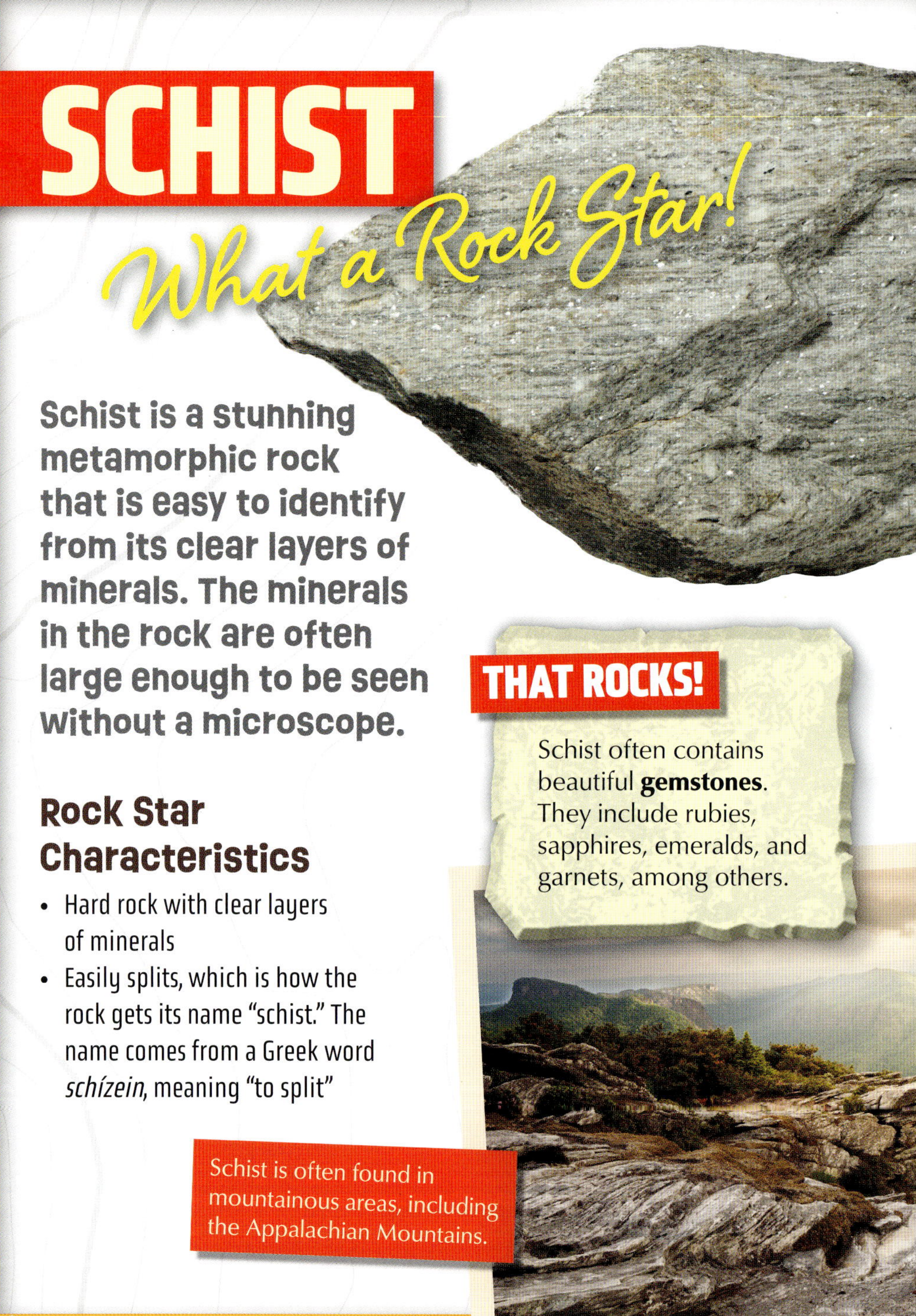

Schist is a stunning metamorphic rock that is easy to identify from its clear layers of minerals. The minerals in the rock are often large enough to be seen without a microscope.

Rock Star Characteristics

- Hard rock with clear layers of minerals
- Easily splits, which is how the rock gets its name "schist." The name comes from a Greek word *schízein*, meaning "to split"

THAT ROCKS!

Schist often contains beautiful **gemstones**. They include rubies, sapphires, emeralds, and garnets, among others.

Schist is often found in mountainous areas, including the Appalachian Mountains.

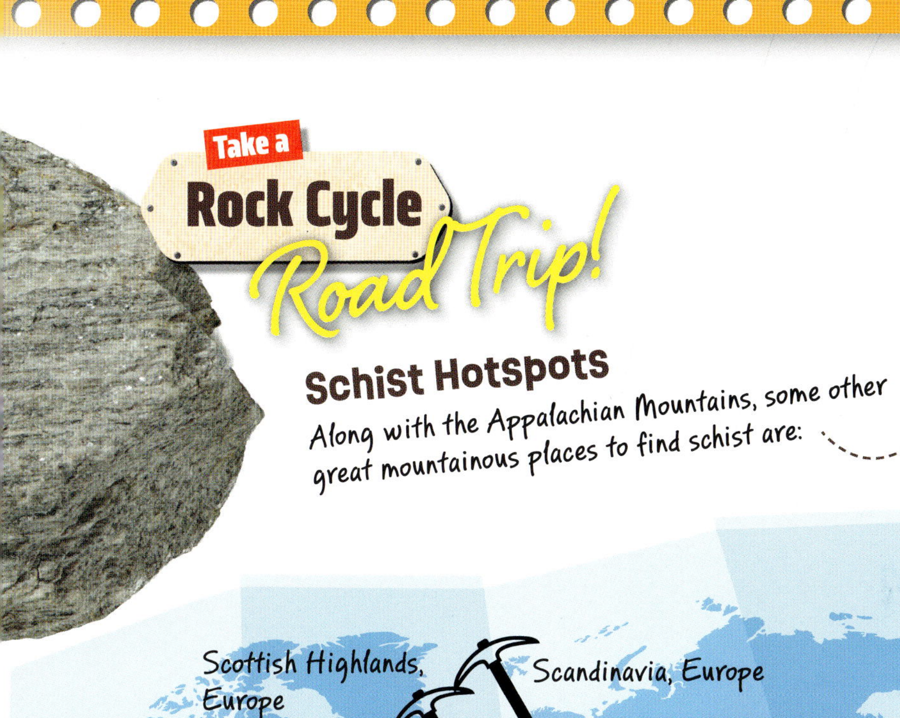

Schist Hotspots

Along with the Appalachian Mountains, some other great mountainous places to find schist are:

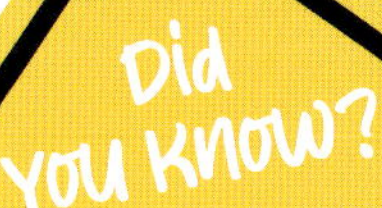

Chapter 2

Heat and Pressure

Miles and miles beneath Earth's surface, it becomes much hotter and the pressure increases greatly. In these conditions, new rocks are created from existing minerals.

Getting Hotter

Did you know that ice begins to melt when the surrounding temperature reaches 32 degrees Fahrenheit (0 °C) or above. The same process takes place with minerals, but at far higher temperatures. The farther a rock travels beneath Earth's surface, the closer it gets to Earth's incredibly hot core. Near this hot center, the minerals in rock melt and change form.

Feel the Pressure

We measure pressure in bars. The pressure on our bodies at Earth's surface is the downward push of the **atmosphere** above our heads. This measures 1 bar. About 20 miles (32 km) underground, the pressure measures an incredible 10,000 bars. This huge pressure is created by the downward push of the heavy rock above, and that pressure can make the minerals in rocks change.

Earth's incredibly hot interior heats underground water, which is forced out of the surface by intense pressure. That creates a spout of hot water known as a geyser.

Changing Times

Rocks at Earth's surface are very hard because the minerals inside them are solid. Beneath Earth's surface, nearer to the core, rocks are heated up. They are also squashed by the weight of other rocks above and around them. Pressure and heat change the minerals in rocks. The rocks then transform, or change, into another type of rock. Metamorphic rocks can form anywhere on Earth where surface rock becomes buried deep enough to change into metamorphic rock.

Digging Deeper

All rocks are made from one or more minerals. In a rock, the minerals are solid. However, in magma, they have melted and bonded together. When magma cools, the different minerals in it each start to form solid, regular-shaped **crystals** that we call grains when identifying rocks.

Under Pressure

Have you ever felt your eardrums pop when you dove under water? That pop was the effect of pressure on your eardrums. Just as they affect your ears, depth and pressure also affect how metamorphic rocks change.

Changing Shapes

When some rocks are pressed hard in one direction, the minerals inside the rocks change shape. Granite is an igneous rock that contains many small minerals. When they are pushed from one direction, all the minerals inside the rock line up and point at **right angles** to the push. This creates a new metamorphic rock called gneiss.

Deeper and Deeper

When one area of Earth's crust dips beneath another, it can travel deeper below the surface. As the rocks in that area of crust gradually move deeper, they change into different types of metamorphic rocks.

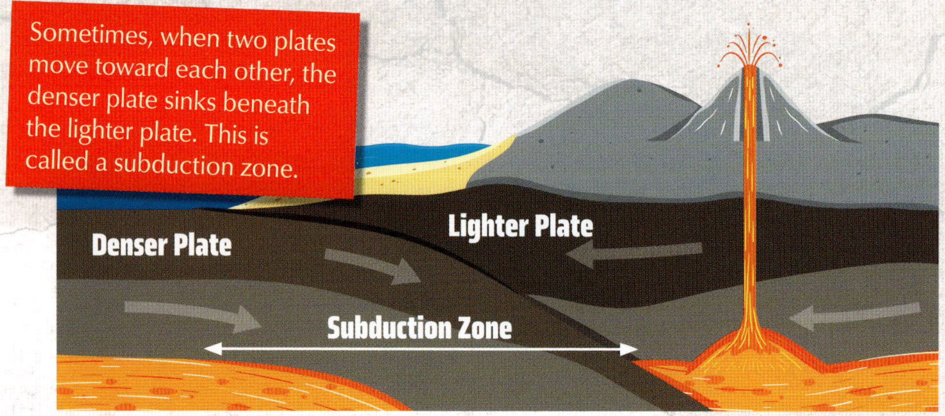

Many Changes

At around 5 miles (8 km) deep, a sedimentary rock called shale turns to a metamorphic rock called slate. At about 8 miles (12.5 km) it turns to phyllite. As it travels even deeper, and gets even hotter, the phyllite rock changes into schist. At around 14 miles (22.5 km) deep, schist turns into gneiss. Even deeper still, the rock changes to another metamorphic rock called migmatite.

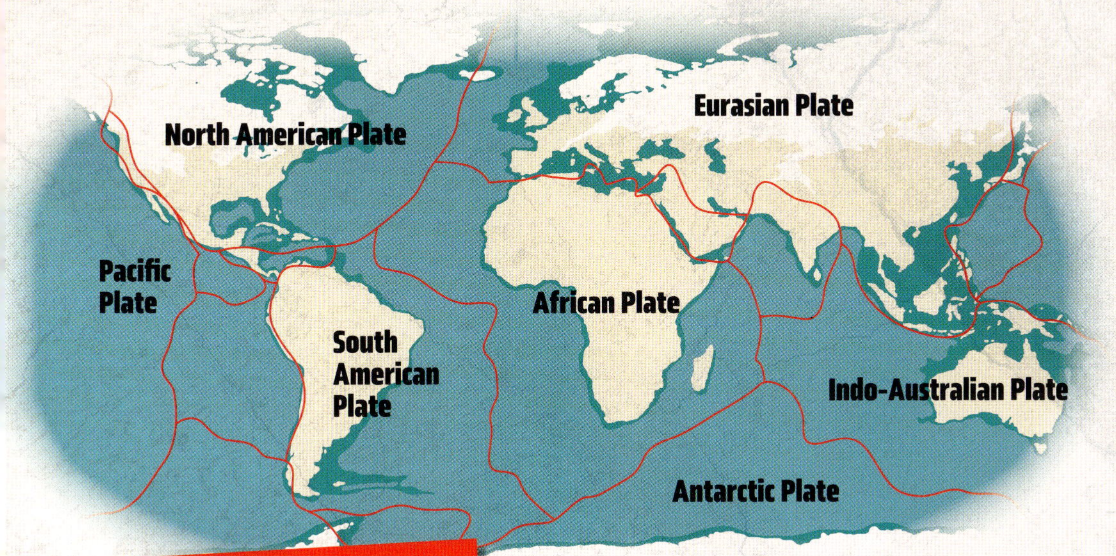

Earth has seven major plates, as shown in this diagram.

Digging Deeper

The plates that make up Earth's crust are called tectonic plates. The biggest plate is the Pacific Plate, which sits beneath the Pacific Ocean. The other major plates are the North and South American, African, Eurasian, Antarctic, and Indo-Australian plates. They sit beneath the world's **continents**. As these plates move, the continents move with them.

History Trail

Some minerals, such as chlorite and muscovite, are formed only at low temperatures and pressures. Others, such as garnet and sillimanite, form only with great heat and pressure. By studying the minerals of metamorphic rocks, scientists can figure out their history.

PHYLLITE

What a Rock Star!

Phyllite is a distinctive metamorphic rock that can be identified by its flake-shaped minerals, which lie **parallel** to one another.

Rock Star Characteristics

- Black, gray, or light green in color
- Easily splits into sheets or slabs
- Crinkled or wavy appearance

THAT ROCKS!

Phyllite is both a soft and durable rock. That makes it easy to cut and shape but also hard-wearing. For that reason, it is often used to make floor tiles and other useful and decorative features.

Phyllite Hotspots

Phyllite is found in many places around the world. Along with the Alps, here are some of the other places it can be spotted:

Phyllite can be found in the Alps of Europe.

Getting into Hot Water

The minerals in some rocks in Earth's crust change quickly when they are touched by hot water. This process often takes place on ocean floors, and it creates metamorphic rocks. Let's discover how.

Water Invasion

One of the places where water often gets deep inside Earth's crust is where plates pull apart. Seawater moves into cracks made in rock as the plates pull away from one another. As the water travels deeper inside the crack, and moves closer to Earth's core, it gets hotter and hotter.

This crack in Earth's crust lies underwater at a point where two plates pull apart off the coast of Iceland, Europe.

Causing Changes

When water becomes extremely hot, it can dissolve minerals and cause **chemical** changes in rocks. For example, hot water that gets into tiny cracks in granite can dissolve minerals rich in iron. It makes red metamorphic rock along these cracks because a new mineral called **hematite** forms there.

Chimneys in the Ocean

Strange-looking structures are dotted across parts of the ocean floor. They look a little like chimneys. These structures form naturally around volcanic vents, or holes, in Earth's crust. They are created when high pressure inside Earth forces hot mineral solutions to spurt up through the crust, into the ocean above. When the solutions hit the cold seawater, they cool. The cooling turns the minerals in the solutions, such as copper and iron, into crystals. These crystals then gradually build up in chimney shapes around the hole in the ocean floor.

Take a
Rock Cycle
Road Trip!

The Mid-Atlantic Ridge is an area where plates pull apart and magma rises to Earth's surface, and it's the next stop on our road trip. Head this way!

ROCK STOP! **THE MID-ATLANTIC RIDGE, ATLANTIC OCEAN**

The Mid-Atlantic Ridge, which runs down the center of the Atlantic Ocean, is about 10,000 miles (16,000 km) long, making it the longest mountain range on our planet. However, most of it is found beneath the waves! The ridge lies on a line where plates meet and magma comes to the surface. As it cools, the magma creates new crust at a rate of around 1 inch (2.5 cm) per year. As a result, the mountain range continually grows.

Some of the mountains of the Mid-Atlantic Ridge reach above **sea level** and form islands, or groups of islands. They include Iceland (shown left), the Azores, Ascension, St. Helena, and Tristan da Cunha islands, among others.

Metamorphic Stars

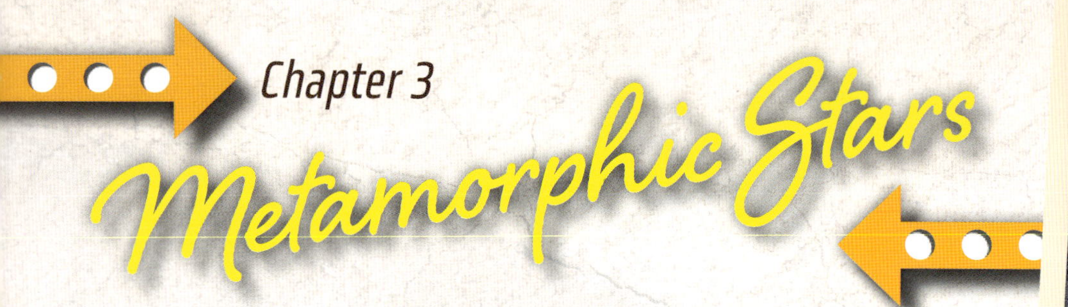

Metamorphic rocks cover around 12 percent of Earth's land surface, and these changeable rocks can be both useful and decorative. Let's look at some more of the metamorphic stars.

A Muddy Start

Slate is a metamorphic rock that forms from mud containing a lot of clay. That mudstone (shale) was squashed under huge pressure and heated up when Earth's plates pushed together around 300 to 400 million years ago. Clay contains a mineral called mica. Under pressure, mica forms narrow crystals in sheets at right angles to the direction of the pressure. It is along the gaps between these sheets that slate can be easily broken.

A Popular Rock Star

Slate is one of the most widely used metamorphic rocks on Earth, mainly because it can be easily split into pieces. For hundreds of years, people have used thin sheets of slate to waterproof the roofs of buildings.

Penrhyn Quarry in Wales was once the largest slate mine in the world. Today, it is the site of an amazing ziplining activity center.

Some of the best-quality slate in the world is from Wales in the UK. Head this way to check out this Welsh wonder!

ROCK STOP! WILD WALES, EUROPE

Welsh slate began as mudstone that lay deep on the ancient seafloor that covered the area now known as Wales around 500 million years ago. The rock lifted, folded, and changed into slate about 400 million years ago.

There are three main large areas of slate, known as deposits, in Wales: Cambrian, Ordovician, and Silurian. Cambrian slate is the oldest of all, some was formed 485 million years ago! Ordovician slate dates to around 444 million years ago, while Silurian slate can date back to 419 million years ago.

Welsh slate is one of the hardest, strongest, and longest-lasting slates in the world. The slate easily splits into thin sheets that can be used for tiles. It is especially useful for roofing because it is waterproof and long-lasting.

What a Rock Star!

Slate is often thought to be only gray, but the rock's color depends on the minerals it contains. For example, dark slate usually contains black **iron sulfide**, and red slate usually contains hematite. Green slate contains chlorite, which is a green mineral.

Rock Star Characteristics

- Light or dark gray, green, black, purple, brown, and even red in color
- Easily splits into sheets
- Fine-grained, mainly smooth appearance

Did You Know?

In the 1800s, elementary school children used a small piece of slate that was framed in wood for writing practice and math. A small pencil made of slate or soapstone was used to make marks on the framed slate. It was wiped clean with a wet cloth.

Slate Hotspots

Slate is also easy to spot in these places:

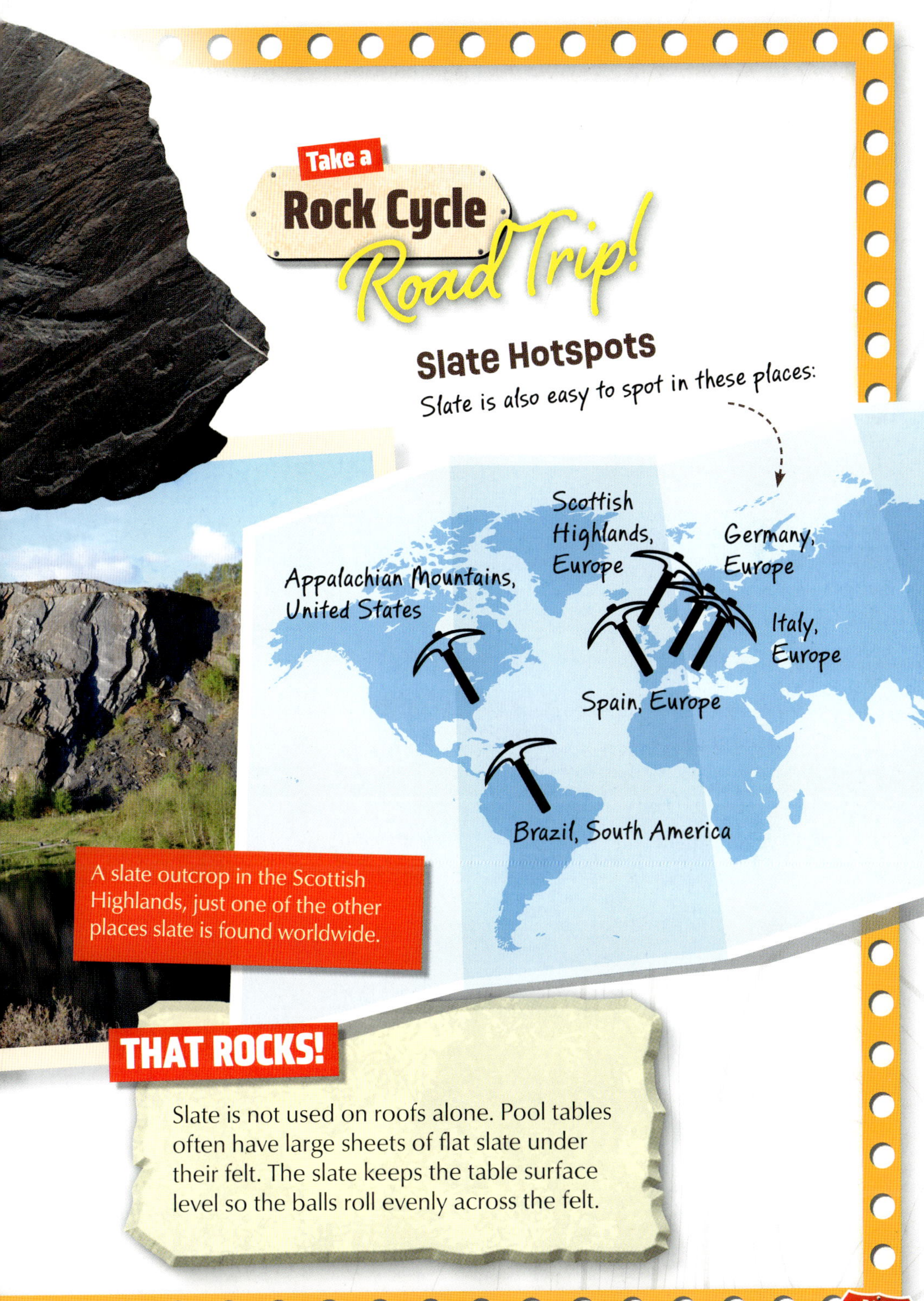

A slate outcrop in the Scottish Highlands, just one of the other places slate is found worldwide.

THAT ROCKS!

Slate is not used on roofs alone. Pool tables often have large sheets of flat slate under their felt. The slate keeps the table surface level so the balls roll evenly across the felt.

Sedimentary Start

Marble is another metamorphic wonder. It begins life as the sedimentary rock limestone. This rock is filled with a mineral called calcite. Intense pressure over long periods of time make the mineral melt. It then turns into multishaped, interlocking, or joined, crystals, which make the marble much harder than the original sedimentary rock. The colors in marble are caused by **impurities** in the crystals.

A Rock Bake

Most marble forms when Earth's plates push into each other. However, some forms when lumps of incredibly hot magma rise through rock nearer Earth's surface. This bakes the limestone in the rock into marble. Marble formed this way usually has smaller calcite grains than that formed by large movements in Earth's crust.

Some of the most famous buildings, monuments, and works of art in the world are made of marble, and they are the next stops on our road trip. Head this way!

MARBLE AROUND THE WORLD

There are many amazing buildings that have been made from marble, because this rock is so dazzling. When the ancient Greeks built the Parthenon in Athens, they wanted to make a building that outshone any other temple ever built—so they used marble! The Parthenon is so stunning that it inspired many other marble structures around the world, including the Supreme Court and the Lincoln Memorial in the United States.

The Dome of the Rock in Israel, in the Middle East, is one of the most famous holy sites on Earth. It was built in the seventh century and decorated with marble and **mosaics**.

One of the most famous marble buildings by far is the Taj Mahal in India, Asia. It is made from white marble and **precious stones** and is believed to be one of the most beautiful buildings in the world.

The famous Italian artist Michelangelo created the *David* sculpture between 1501 and 1504. It was carved from a single slab of white marble.

MARBLE

What a Rock Star!

Few rocks are as beautiful and easy to work with as marble. Although this metamorphic rock star is hard, it is easy to cut.

Rock Star Characteristics

- Reflects light well because of its tight crystal structure
- Pure marble is white, but marble can also be blue, gray, pink, yellow, or black
- Can be polished to show off its stunning veins, or lines, and swirls of color

THAT ROCKS!

The word "marble" comes from a Greek word, *marmar*. It means "to shine." Many ancient Greek and Roman sculptors (artists who create objects by carving them from stone) used marble to create sculptures.

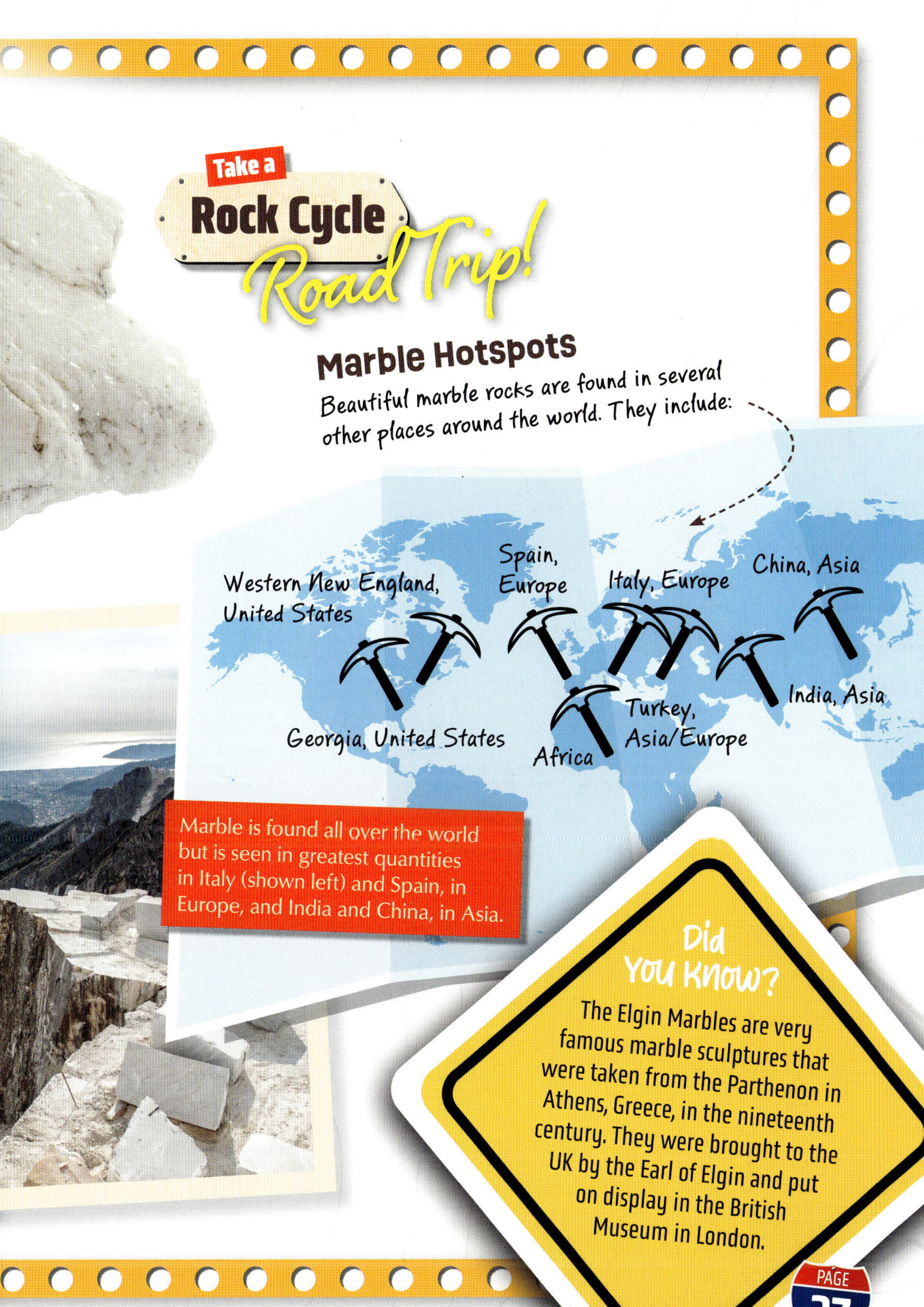

Marble Hotspots

Beautiful marble rocks are found in several other places around the world. They include:

Marble is found all over the world but is seen in greatest quantities in Italy (shown left) and Spain, in Europe, and India and China, in Asia.

Did You Know?

The Elgin Marbles are very famous marble sculptures that were taken from the Parthenon in Athens, Greece, in the nineteenth century. They were brought to the UK by the Earl of Elgin and put on display in the British Museum in London.

Rock Band

One of the most common metamorphic rocks, gneiss, has bands that run through it. The bands in gneiss can be either incredibly obvious or are so small they can only be seen using a microscope. Whatever the size, the bands tell us how the rock formed.

Hot Rocks

Of all the metamorphic rocks, gneiss has some of the biggest grains. This proves that, like marble, gneiss forms at very high temperatures. At high temperatures, some mineral grains dissolve, making room for other mineral grains to grow bigger. In gneiss, the large mineral grains are also arranged in bands, because the rock forms at very high pressures. The lighter bands are often made of **quartz** and feldspar minerals.

When gneiss is pushed in one direction, it folds and twists. The bands in gneiss are not always even and may be twisted. This proves that the rock was pushed in the direction of the bands after they had been formed.

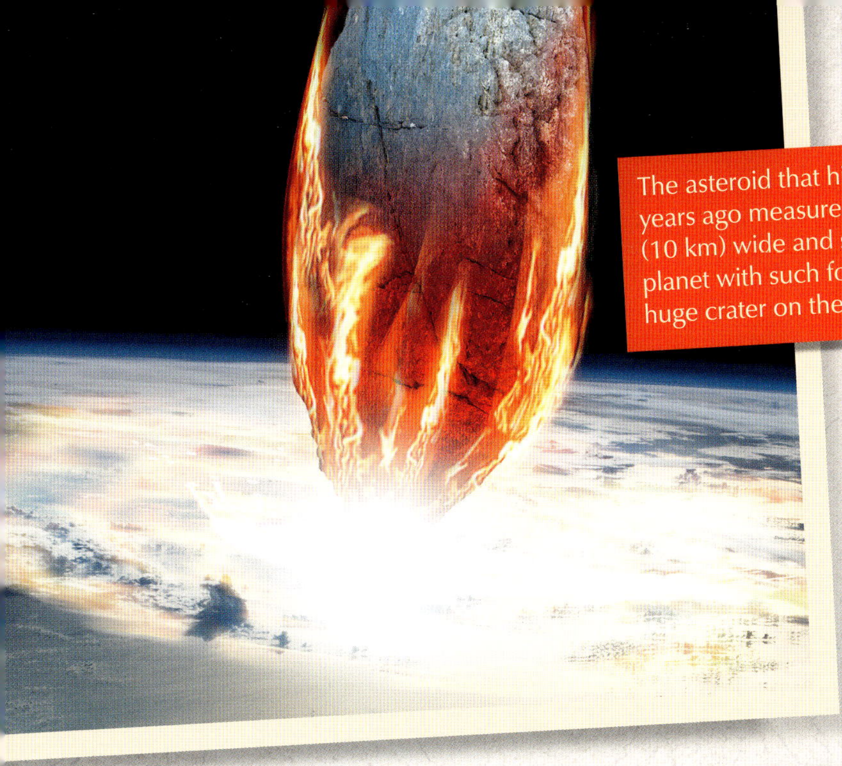

The asteroid that hit Earth 66 million years ago measured about 6 miles (10 km) wide and slammed into the planet with such force that it left a huge crater on the surface.

READ Here

Digging Deeper

Rocks aren't just found on Earth—there are plenty of rocks in space too! There are other rocky planets, and there are also rocks that fly through space such as comets, asteroids, and meteoroids. An asteroid hit Earth about 66 million years ago. The disaster is believed to have led to the **extinction** of the dinosaurs.

Spot That Rock!

Gneiss can be identified by the type of rock from which it formed, the types of minerals it contains, or their shapes. Pencil gneiss has a lot of pencil-shaped minerals running through it. Augen gneiss has mineral lumps that are shaped a little like the lenses of eyes. This is why the rock is called "augen," which means "eyes" in German.

GNEISS

What a Rock Star!

Gneiss is often mistaken for schist, because both types are metamorphic rocks with clear layers. However, gneiss is grainier than schist and does not easily split. Some of the oldest stones discovered on Earth are gneiss stones.

Rock Star Characteristics

- Contains clear layers of mineral grains which are arranged in bands
- Usually contains bands of black, white, pink, or gold
- Has alternating bands of dark and light colors
- Can be polished to show off its stunning velns, or lInes, and swirls of color

A great place to see gneiss is in Australia.

THAT ROCKS!

One of the most famous types of gneiss is often called rainbow granite because it has striking colors and is formed from granite. The Morton Gneiss from Minnesota, has pink, swirling bands running through it. This 3.5 billion-year-old rock is used as a decorative stone.

Take a
Rock Cycle
Road Trip!

Did You Know?

Unlike other metamorphic rocks, gneiss does not usually split in places where the rock is weak. That is why builders often use the tough and durable rock as crushed stone to make roads.

Gneiss Hotspots

Here are some of the other places in the world where gneiss is found:

Rare in Rocks

Many different minerals can be found in a lot of different types of rocks. However, some minerals are very unusual and can be found only in metamorphic rocks.

Talking Talc

Did you know that the talcum powder people sprinkle on themselves after a bath is a ground-up mineral taken from metamorphic rock? Soapstone and serpentinite contain talc. These rocks form deep underground.

Talc is the softest mineral on Earth, because its layers of silicate crystals are only weakly bound together. Ground talc absorbs moisture and people use it to help them dry their bodies.

Digging Deeper

Some valuable minerals within metamorphic rock are found in large deposits in specific places on Earth. For example, jade is a semiprecious stone that is especially valuable in China, where it is used to make sculptures and ornaments.

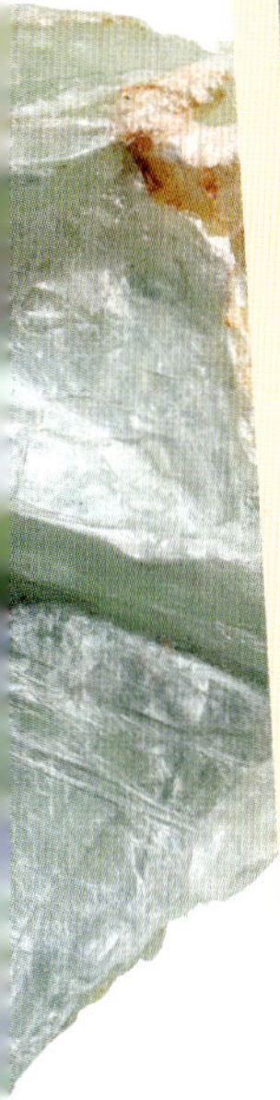

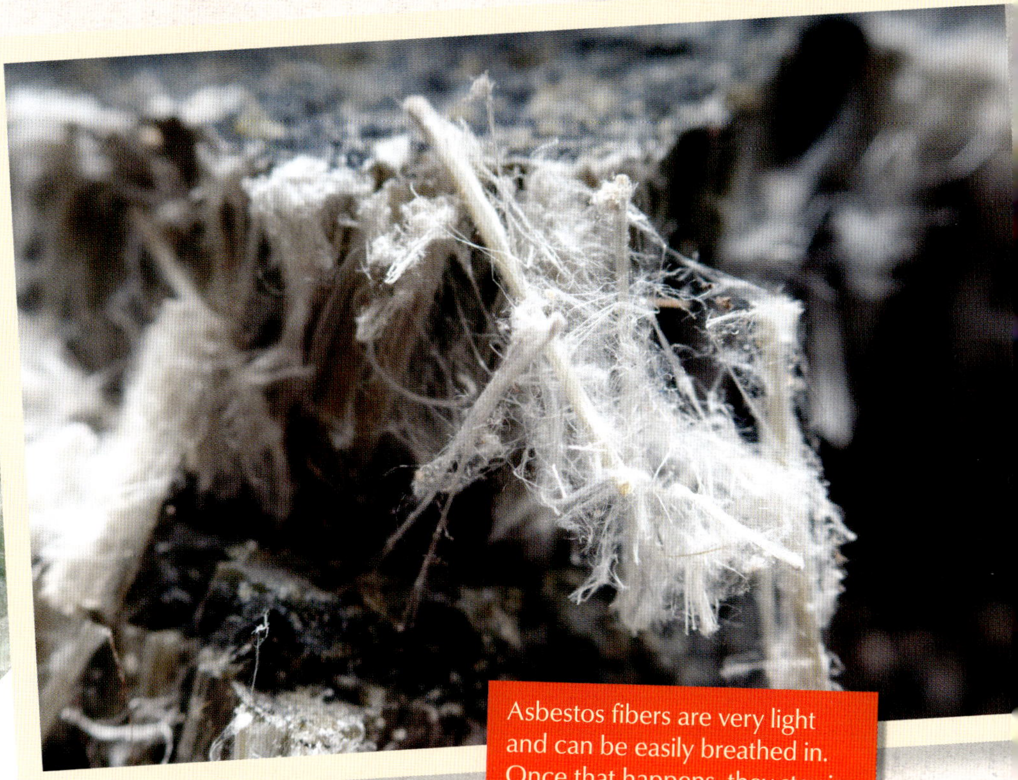

Asbestos fibers are very light and can be easily breathed in. Once that happens, they stay in the body and damage the lungs.

Asbestos Danger

Asbestos is a metamorphic mineral that was once used to make materials that can resist heat, such as pipes. However, asbestos is rarely used today because it is so dangerous to people's health. It has unusually long, thin, straight, or curly crystals that are a little like fabric fibers.

Shattered Rock

Suevite is an unusual metamorphic rock that contains shattered stones and glassy minerals. It is rare because it forms only where meteorites from space hit Earth. Meteorites strike at speeds of up to 400 miles per hour (644 kph). The collision speed causes rock minerals from both the meteorite and the rock on Earth to melt and break. The rock minerals then cool and reform into suevite. The rock is useful because it tells scientists when and where meteorites hit Earth in the past.

SOAPSTONE
What a Rock Star!

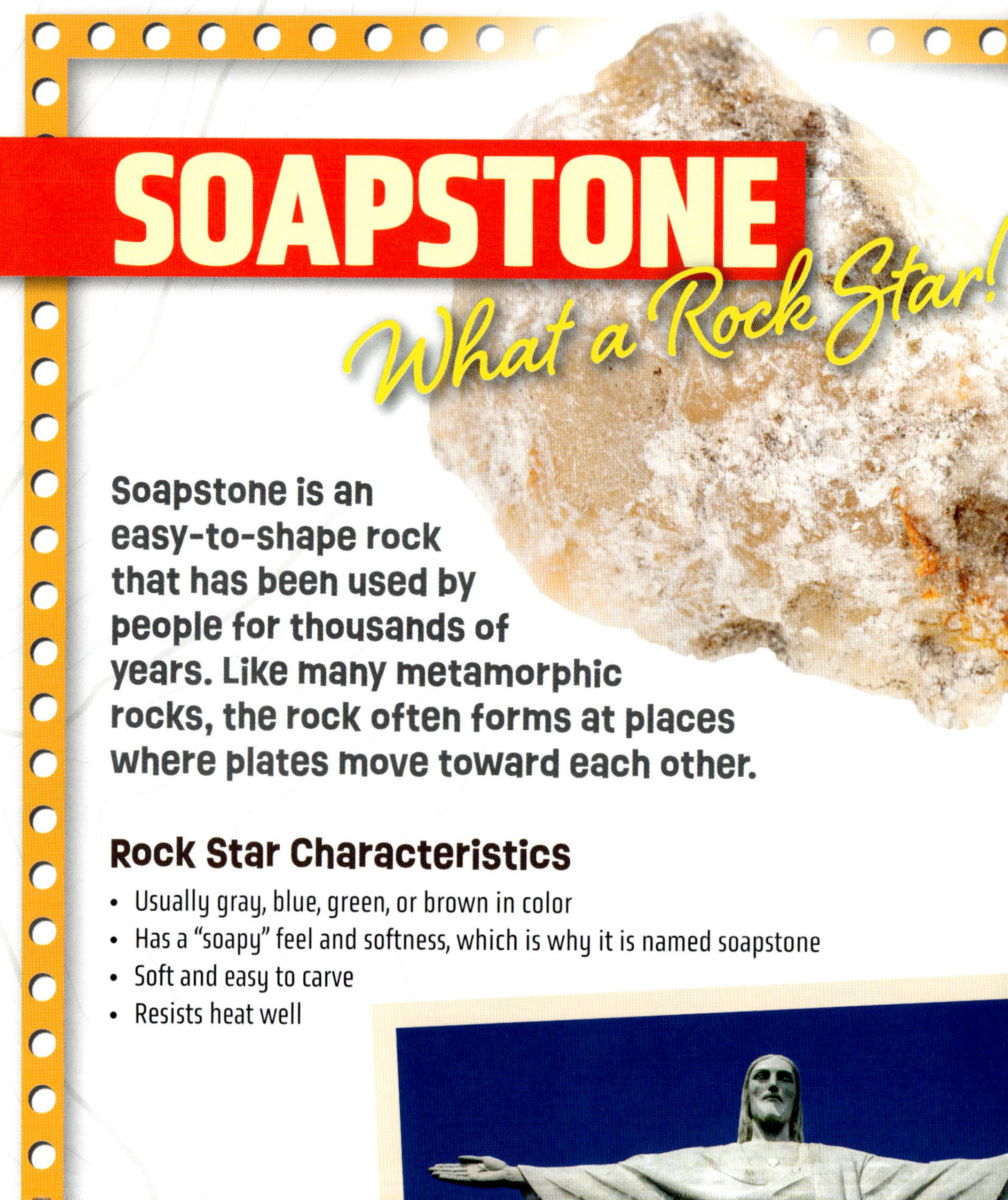

Soapstone is an easy-to-shape rock that has been used by people for thousands of years. Like many metamorphic rocks, the rock often forms at places where plates move toward each other.

Rock Star Characteristics

- Usually gray, blue, green, or brown in color
- Has a "soapy" feel and softness, which is why it is named soapstone
- Soft and easy to carve
- Resists heat well

A lot of the world's soapstone comes from China, India, and Brazil. The famous Christ the Redeemer statue in Rio de Janeiro, in Brazil, is party made of soapstone.

Soapstone Hotspots

Here are places in the world where soapstone is found:

THAT ROCKS!

People have dug out soapstone and used the soft rock for thousands of years. Scandinavian people began to use soapstone during the **Stone Age**, and later discovered that they could carve it into molds from which metal objects such as blades and spearheads could be made. Native Americans also used it to make bowls, smoking pipes, and ornaments.

At the Surface

Sometimes, metamorphic rocks seem to reach Earth's surface as if by magic! That magic is weathering and erosion. Surface rock gradually weathers, for example, when ice freezes in cracks and forces the cracks to grow wider. Rushing rivers, crashing waves, or wild winds can carry or erode surface rock pieces away. This gradually reveals the rocks beneath.

Slow or Fast

The speed at which weathering or erosion of rock takes place depends on the softness of the rocks. Hard lumps of rock can remain even when the softer rock that formed around them has gone. The pieces of rock worn away by weathering and erosion can form new sedimentary rock. This rock may eventually become buried deep beneath Earth's surface, where it turns into new metamorphic rocks.

The Caledonian Mountains once stretched from Greenland through the UK and into the United States. Today you can see the metamorphic rock of the Caledonian Mountains in the Blue Ridge Mountains of Virginia.

Take a
Rock Cycle
Road Trip!

Weathering and erosion causes amazing formations on our planet's surface, and some of the best examples are the Caledonian Mountains and the amazing rock formations in Utah. Head this way!

ROCK STOP! ## THE CALEDONIAN MOUNTAINS AND UTAH

The Caledonian Mountains formed when two ancient continents collided around 450 million years ago, as Earth's plates shifted. Today, much of the top of the Caledonian Mountains has weathered and eroded, but there are a lot of places where the metamorphic rock that formed when the plates collided has now reached the surface.

Utah's Arches National Park is covered in amazing rock formations that have been created over millions of years. Ancient seas covered the area more than 300 million years ago, leaving a layer of salt. Over time, layers of sandstone built up on the salt layer below. The weight of the sandstone caused the salt layer to shift—pushing some of the stone up into amazing dome shapes. Other areas collapsed. Water, ice, and wind then shaped the sandstone into the amazing shapes we see today.

QUARTZITE
What a Rock Star!

Quartzite is an incredibly tough stone that is formed when sandstone is affected by heat and pressure, turning it into quartzite. In the metamorphic process, sandstone's sand grains and **silica** are recrystallized, creating a network of incredibly tight interlocking quartz grains.

THAT ROCKS!

More than 1 million years ago, people used quartzite to make stone tools. The rock was mainly used to make cutting and chopping tools such as axes, scrapers, and **hoes**.

Quartzite is found in many parts of the United States, from South Dakota, Minnesota, and Utah through Wisconsin, Texas, Pennsylvania, Arizona, and California. The famous Pipestone National Monument in Minnesota (above) is made of quartzite.

Rock Star Characteristics

- Usually white or gray in color, but can be stained pink, red, purple, yellow, orange, brown, green, or blue when iron or impurities come into contact with the rock
- Extremely tough
- Can resist chemicals and even harsh weathering

Take a
Rock Cycle
Road Trip!

Quartzite Hotspots

Here are some of the other places in the world where quartzite is found:

Metamorphic Miracle

Metamorphic rocks are important parts of our planet's surface and provide vital resources, or things that we use and rely on. We use metamorphic rocks in so many areas of our lives that it is difficult to imagine a world without them.

Stories in Rocks

Metamorphic rocks are fascinating because their minerals, shapes, and structures are a record of the huge changes going on all the time underground. They show us what the great heat and pressure deep inside our planet can do. Metamorphic rocks reveal how the boiling pot of heat and pressure inside Earth is constantly changing our planet. The rocks also help us date areas of our planet.

Rich Resources

Slate, marble, talc, gneiss, and other metamorphic rocks are important resources for building. However, the amazing metamorphic rocks that form mountains and cliffs come under threat when people dig up too much stone. So too do the organisms that live near them. For example, deep-ocean places are under threat because people want to mine the metamorphic minerals near vents. Scientists have discovered many unusual animals around the vents, which can survive in very deep waters. They include clams, mussels, crabs, fish, octopuses, and giant tube worms. All these creatures will be threatened if metamorphic minerals are mined near the vents.

Digging Deeper

Deep-sea vents can appear incredibly quickly. In fact, they can grow up to 30 feet (9 m) in just 18 months. One vent in the Pacific Ocean, off the coast of Oregon, is known as "Godzilla." That is because it reached the height of a 15-story building before it collapsed!

Rocks Forever?

Although new metamorphic rock is forming all the time, this process is very slow. We need to keep this in mind when we make use of Earth's rock cycle. If we use too much of our planet's precious metamorphic rock, too quickly, we could run out of this vital resource.

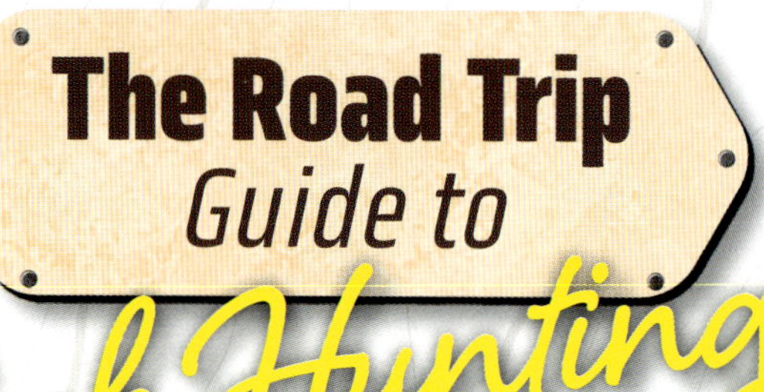

The Road Trip Guide to Rock Hunting

Had a great road trip? Loved the book? Want to try out rock hunting yourself? Awesome! Here's an easy guide that will explain the basics. The great thing about hunting for rocks is that anyone can do it and it costs very little. All you need is a pair of sharp eyes and some resources such as books and websites to help you identify the rocks. A few key pieces of kit help too.

Hammer and Chisel

The rock hunter's most important tools are a hammer and chisel—and it's worth investing in some proper geological ones. The hammer should mostly be used for splitting stones, and not for breaking stones from cliff faces.

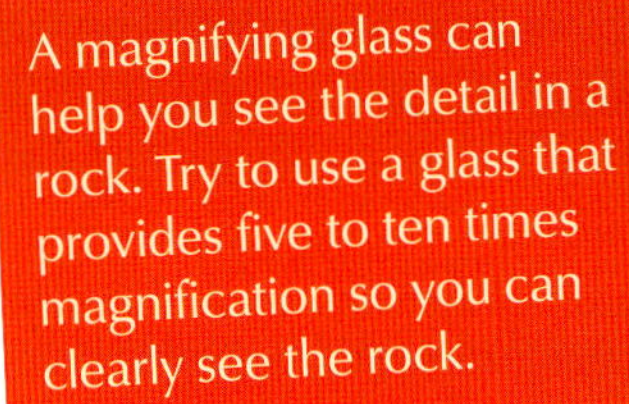

A magnifying glass can help you see the detail in a rock. Try to use a glass that provides five to ten times magnification so you can clearly see the rock.

ROCK CLUES

Use these questions to help you identify common metamorphic rocks:

- Do they have bands or layers? If the answer is yes, the rocks are probably slate (has thin layers), schist, or gneiss (has dark and white bands). If the answer is no, the rocks are probably marble or quartzite.
- How big are the grains in the rock? If they are small, the rock is probably slate. If they are large, it is gneiss or schist.
- Are the rocks hard enough to scratch glass? If the answer is yes, the rock is quartzite, gneiss, or schist. If the answer is no, the rock could be slate or marble.

Keep safe!

Rocks can be sharp, heavy, and hard, and the places where you find them may be dangerous, so it's very important to keep safe. Try to rock hunt in a group and take an adult with you. Rocks can splinter when hit, so always wear goggles when hammering. Tough gloves are useful and a helmet is also important for protection if working near places where rocks could fall.

Geologists always wear safety equipment such as a helmet and goggles when searching for rocks.

QUIZ

How much have you learned about metamorphic rocks, the rock cycle, and our amazing planet on your road trip? Take the quiz and find out!

1. What does the word "metamorphic" mean?

2. What three layers make up Earth?

3. What is the tallest mountain in the world?

4. What stones does schist often contain?

5. What are deep-sea vents?

6. What is the world's longest mountain range?

7. What metamorphic rock is Wales famous for?

8. What metamorphic rock is the Taj Mahal made of?

9. Along with metamorphic rock, what other two types of rock exist on Earth?

10. How do rocks break down on Earth's surface?

ANSWERS

1. A change in form
2. The crust, mantle, and core
3. Mount Everest
4. Gemstones
5. Openings in Earth's crust on the seabed, through which hot mineral solutions escape
6. The Mid-Atlantic Ridge
7. Slate
8. Marble
9. Igneous and sedimentary
10. By weathering and erosion

GLOSSARY

atmosphere the layers of gases that surround Earth or another planet

chemical a substance that has a particular composition. Chemical erosion can cause some rocks to wear away

collisions when moving objects strike violently against other objects

continents continuous expanses of land on Earth. The seven continents are Asia, Africa, North America, South America, Antarctica, Europe, and Oceania

crystals minerals that have a very ordered arrangement of atoms in regular, repeating, symmetrical patterns. When we identify rocks, we call the crystals "grains"

earthquake when the movement of Earth's crust causes a sudden release of energy and the ground shakes at the surface

elements substances that cannot be broken down into simpler substances by chemical means

extinction the complete disappearance of a species from Earth

gemstones minerals that can be cut and polished and used as jewelry

geologists scientists who study Earth and what it is made of

hematite a reddish-brown to black mineral found in rocks and soils

hoes tools with a thin metal blade, used to clear soil

impurities substances found in small quantities in another substance, making it less pure

iron sulfide a black-brown mineral that contains iron and sulfur

minerals substances formed by natural geological processes on Earth. All rocks are made from one or more minerals

mosaics decorative pictures or patterns made by arranging small pieces of stone

parallel lying side by side, with the same distance between

precious stones rare and valuable minerals, often used as jewelry. There are four precious stones—diamond, sapphire, ruby, and emerald. Less valuable jewelry may contain semiprecious stones

pressure a continuous physical force exerted on an object by something it is in contact with. Pressure increases underground, for example, because of the downward push of rock above

quartz a hard mineral commonly found in Earth's crust. Quartz mainly contains silica

raw materials basic materials that occur naturally on Earth that are used or processed to make different products

reflect to throw light back from a surface. Minerals that reflect light are shiny

right angles angles of 90 degrees, such as the corner of a square

sea level the level of the sea's surface. Sea level is used to determine the height of geographical features, such as hills and mountains

silica the main component of quartz. Silica is also found in sedimentary rocks such as sandstone

Solar System our Sun and the planets and other bodies that orbit it

Stone Age a prehistoric period which began about 2.6 million years ago, when weapons and tools were made from stone or other natural materials such as bone or horn

weathering the wearing away of a substance over time because of the effects of sunlight, wind, water, or other weather conditions

Books

Fretland VanVoorst, Jennifer. *Metamorphic Rocks* (True Books). Scholastic, 2020.

Rogers, Marie. *Exploring Metamorphic Rocks* (Let's Rock!). Rosen Publishing Group, 2022.

Woolf, Alex. *The Science of Rocks and Minerals: The Hard Truth About the Stuff Beneath Our Feet.* Scholastic, 2018.

Websites

Take another look at the rock cycle at:
www.cotf.edu/ete/modules/msese/earthsysflr/rock.html

Test your knowledge about rocks at the DK website:
www.dkfindout.com/uk/earth/rocks-and-mlnerals

Discover more about metamorphic rocks at:
education.nationalgeographic.org/resource/metamorphic-rocks

Learn all about minerals, crystals, and other aspects of rocks at:
www.mineralogy4kids.org

Publisher's note to educators and parents:
All the websites featured above have been carefully reviewed to ensure that they are suitable for students. However, many websites change often, and we cannot guarantee that a site's future contents will continue to meet our high standards of educational value. Please be advised that students should be closely monitored whenever they access the Internet.

ABOUT THE AUTHOR

Sarah Eason has written many books for children on a wide variety of topics, from history to geography and science. She would love to take a rock cycle road trip and visit some of the amazing rocky places explored in this book.